MILLION LAST GOODBYES

KEROLIN JIVRAJANI

To my Mum – who left me too soon, but never really left me.

I always asked, "Will you ever leave me one day?"

With shimmer in your eyes, you said, "Where would I go leaving you?"

And four years later, here it is. You are every word, every silence, every feather that falls when the wind pauses just long enough to whisper your name.

Contents

Contents

Contents

Contents

Acknowledgements

To grief — You taught me to speak even when the world had nothing left to say. You gave me the Crow, the silences, the panic, the longing, the feathers, and the words.

To everyone who has ever sat quietly with loss — Thank you for understanding that this isn't a book, it's a pulse worth living. To those who offered warmth when I felt I would never feel again, you gave me my voice back.

To *Tanmayee Kawali* — thank you for helping me shape these words with care and intention. To *Anamika Gupta* and *Malavika Saji* — for being constant, patient, and never letting me forget that I still had pieces worth gathering.

To my readers — If you have loved and lost, these pages are yours as much as they are mine. May they sit beside you like a quiet friend.

And to Death — This is the closest I'll ever come to understanding you. Please don't come again too soon.

Prologue

I didn't mean to write a book. I only meant to express.

I meant to hold her hand again, or find the echo of her laugh somewhere between the sheets. I meant to remember her exactly as she was or maybe how I wanted her to be or thought her to be, but memory is slippery and grief keeps rearranging the scenes. So I started writing — not because I was brave, but because I was breaking. I wrote in pieces, in crumbs, in conversations with the Crow and the dark. I wrote like I was still asking for her to come back. I still keep pining for her.

This isn't a manual. It doesn't move in neat chapters or offer neat truths. Grief didn't come to me like that, and I don't think it ever will. What's here are the fragments — soft, sharp, heavy, light — of a love that never really left. I stitched them together because I needed to, not because I knew how to.

If you are here, maybe you've lost someone too. Maybe you're speaking to the ceiling fan, or looking for signs in feathers, or folding their clothes slower than usual. Maybe you're holding on to their scent, their brush, and their pillow. Maybe you're wondering how to live with the absence and the presence all at once.

I don't have answers. I only have this. A small place where our goodbyes don't have to be final.

1

Sitting in the Garden.

Even as I write this, I feel a strange insincerity in me. It's as if my conscience tells me to keep it to myself—no one would really understand. *No one experiences grief in such an exaggerated manner*, my brain tells me. It keeps saying that you're not with me too, Maa. Who should I believe?

There's an edge of insanity in grief. It doesn't just rotate; it revolves around you. In one moment, I feel nothing, and in the next, a turmoil—a hurricane of intense emotions I can't even identify with. With grief comes this great capacity to numb, and to numb is to feel—maybe too much for the heart to even conceal.

The blades of this grass cut deep, piercing through the insanity of this existence, crossing their edges through my skin. *How did you slip away?* I still ask myself. Would being there with you have saved you? Would my life have meant anything to you, Maa? Did you ever think of the evening we spent together when I walked into the hospital and said, *Mumma?*

Was that ECG meter going up for once before stopping—a sign for me? What were you trying to tell me in that call of blabbers, Maa? Why did you isolate me with this grief?

2

The Opening.

I dreamt your eyes opened this morning, and I found myself still asleep, clutching your kurta in my hands—draped around me as if it were mine. I don't know how I feel. I just know that this is not okay.

You know that dark, deep-down place that mocks us? The one that feels like a crow swooped down, devoured the flesh, and threw aside the bones—while you're starving. That's how it feels. I am alive, but I am also dead.

The crow looks at me with that menacing glare, claiming you as his. He mocks me, maa. He says you belong to him now. I don't know what to do.

The child within me is still sleeping. I love her so much, but she never looks back at me. Once, on her birthday, she gave me a flower. Just that. No more. I tell her good morning every time I see her, maa. She never replies. And sometimes, I wonder—*is she dead, too?*

This moment feels like an opening - so full of love, but it is peeling like an onion—layer by layer, sinking deeper into the abyss. I see you. You're looking at me. Then I wake up. The deadly, drowning feeling sets in me, the abuse of energy is going to take place to survive this day. With this, I clown up to earn that meagre portion of the day to sustain myself.

For no one in the world knows what it's like to have a plant without roots. It'll float, rootless, forever.

3

She's Dead.

What does that even mean? Communicate? Communicate with whom? Where on earth shall I address her letter to—you, crow? Speak now, won't you? Ah, no, you don't like it when people retaliate. You just like to suck their blood dry and leave them cold.

You never feared the girl who never cried, for you knew she had already died inside when she didn't pour. She had nothing to hold on to—she fell into the abyss of nothingness, where even grass doesn't grow. She drowned in apathy. She cried, but no one saw her. She swam, but there was no water. She climbed, but there was no mountain. She searched, but there was no finish.

And so, one day, she decided to leave.

She's gone forever now.

She doesn't know where her mother is or where she could be, but she can smell her in the nightgowns she wore. She can feel her in the kurtas she left behind. She doesn't remember the sound of her mother's voice, but she hears her in the silence. She doesn't hallucinate, but she sees her when she really prays for it.

No, she isn't alive. She died with her mother long ago.

4

The Crow.

I sit among the bereaved, watching them wrestle with their fragile lives. Oh, how I relish the way hope fails them every day. Sweetie, that person isn't ever going to knock on that door and you look stupid waiting for it. I smile.

How naive these humans can be! You curse me, vilify me, but am I not the one who gives you an existence, a purpose to live for? No one is ready when I come, nobody welcomes me. Embrace me and see the magic.

No, it's not those children's fault. It's not yours, either. And it certainly isn't mine. Hey, don't be pissed at me - I'm just doing my job. You clutch the graves so tight and deep; I bury them for you. Those hearts you say torment you? I end their suffering. I kill them so they can't hurt you anymore. Shouldn't you be grateful for that?

My feathers are scattered across the world; I am everywhere and nowhere at once. It's the same story, the same broken script, no matter where I land. Crocodile tears. Sleepless nights. Hollow speeches and off-key songs (oh, how they grate on me). And then the ceremony—a desperate attempt at closure that forgets the very people who need it the most.

I stay behind, picking up the leftovers of your grief. And what remains are the haunting questions, the echo of innocent eyes staring back at me, pleading for answers. And then there's the one—the child who was too wrecked to not cry.

5

Proof Of Her Death.

The crow enters my life every morning as I open my eyes—without blemishes, without concern. It is fearless, unashamed. It leaves its black, utterly dark feathers around the home. On the sofa, on the chair, the table, the spoons, the napkins—everywhere.

It haunts me, just like that day when we opened the house without our family. Just the three of us, ancillary puppets in the game.

The crow hovered as we moved toward the house. Up until then, while we were at others' homes, performing the rituals, it all still felt unreal. Afterall, you chose not to die here, for this mere house could not contain you.

And now, the melody of birds turned into screaming nightmares, stripping away the last grains of strength—slipping through my hands like sand.

The wheels screeched against the road. The tires went flat. A police officer stood waiting for us, asking for proof of your death before letting us cross the border. He didn't see the pain in our eyes or the scalp now bare of hair. He didn't see the weight of loss. Instead, he asked for a piece of paper.

How do I tell him that it's not just my mother who has passed away, but also my childhood, my toffees, my humanity—buried alongside her?

We checked our belongings a million times, making sure we hadn't forgotten anything—because we couldn't bear to place those awkward keys back in the door.

Then came the silence. The silence before the storm.

Dust from the flooding water clung to the doorstep, carrying everything away—from dusk to dawn, from the glow of the stars to the light of the moon.

The crow finally croaked.

And we stood, *numb.*

6

Not a Day That Goes By…

The broken promises mend, the ruthless becomes compassionate, but your body refuses to take any form of life for me. When I smell the armpits of your kurta, I recollect how warm your hug felt—it is your scent that takes me back to you. I feel like I live in a little world with you when I hold that cloth. For a moment, everything about your death feels false, and all my fantasies of having you by my side become true. But the wood of the bed is my enemy. It tries to erase you, pouring itself into the stitches, fading you away.

There's not a day that goes by when I don't see you.

But there's not a day when I find you.

In these broken strands of memories, in this life of grief, maybe we are not meant to be together—but within each other. A part of me was buried with you, and maybe that was my childhood. I don't just long for you; I long for her—to come back once, to feel herself again. But how do I let her, without the safety of your presence?

As if the world wasn't already made of thorns, God decided to pluck away my sunflower. The rose won't grow back, just as the dead won't rise from the tomb. No, I still miss you, Maa—I only ache for you. I only crave you. I only weep for you.

7

Dead, Maybe?

Having feelings for you wasn't just natural, maa—it was wired into me, a genetic disposition. Growing inside you was the safest place I'd ever know, and love. You set me free, and now I'm afraid it's time for me to set you free too.

I am scared. Afraid. Wrenched and worn out from life without you, and yet, I have been living it. Living the worst fear is torment. It's not just waves crashing onto the shore; it's being stuck in a tsunami. I don't know where the waves are coming from, how they are circling wildly, or when these holes in my boat dug themselves. All I know is the flooding. Big waters. Small boat.

I know you are waiting. And I shall keep you there too, for I don't know what else to do. Swimming—I never learned. Yearning—you never taught. But now they are both here for us to take on. How will we?

Was letting me go this easy, maa? Didn't that breath feel heavy? Are you okay where you are?

Waiting won't be a fair trade for your answer. I'd say I'm drowning in the anxiety, in the fear, in the wait for you. I have begun to die, bit by bit, waiting for you.

I hope the rebirth is beautiful. Like a butterfly. As I close my cocoon.

8
Maybe We Should Just Move Forward.

It's been more than a year and a half. All the festivals have passed once now and we know or maybe we'd like to believe that we know how it's going to feel, as if there is anything to feel.

What do your birthdays mean anymore? Are they meant to be celebrated? I don't know what Diwali represents now; it's just flickers of lights, shadows dancing where joy once lived. And oh, how shitty it feels as Christmas is approaching. It isn't that bad really, it's just... as if a knife is cutting through the blackness of my soul tightly every day, trying to get some light, only to find a dark, hollow yet deeply filled suffocating pile of empty black.

And yes, with this... maybe we should just accept it and move forward. After all, that's all that the world wants. Move forward. Move forward. Move forward.

9

Let's Just Pray For Moving On, Shall We?

Yes. Yes, I'm back. I know you hate me the most. After all, I am the one who took away that love from your life and granted them eternal peace. Oh, you've no clue on how marvellous death can be, it frees you from all your suffering. It's gorgeous, actually, but you won't see it that way, would you? The calm in death is just like the one before the storm – only this time, the storm comes to the living ones. For the dead, there's only peace.

You wake up every morning to kiss them, but you can't find them. You look inside the little box of your memories and then snap back to reality, only to notice that they no longer exist. Then you question if they even ever existed. On some occasions, I make memories better for your grief as they cut through you with the pictures of the dead. Memories once posted as family, love, and joy are now shattered, dark and scary.

Hey look, the universe is miserable. It isn't that pretty anymore, especially not when you see the hospital bed or the accident. She wasn't singing on the last day in the car honey. She was living the last day with you. She chose it. Do you truly believe that?

Churches, temples, mosques. God. Gods. You go to all of them to find her, to find some piece of her. Why don't you just look at your face? Why don't you look at your heart? Why don't you look at your damn hair? It's the same, I promise. And sweetie, a little part of you also died that day when you were too full to not cry, to not scream, to not shut down, to not believe that it is indeed the truth.

Well, the chapter is called 'Let's Pray for the Moving On,' and I'd pray for it. Father God, let me be with them for some more time as they process it. Amen. You didn't like this prayer, did you?

10

Christmas is Coming.

Mumma and I celebrated Christmas together. She'd take me to a nearby church, specifically on December 25 - not the 24th because it was too crowded, and we never understood the candlelight service. Coming from a Hindu family and yet having a strange connection to Christ was something only she accepted. She supported me in all I did. How could a mother not accept her child's connection? Maybe she felt it too - maybe with someone else. Oh, I can only speculate now. I wish I had asked her.

It's a lonely Christmas this year. My father neither believes nor is interested in celebrating Christmas with me. As the day approaches, I remember how Mumma would give me a gift only if I put a right-leg sock by my bed (I figured much later that there is no specific "right leg sock"). I'd be her Santa and she'd be my Claus. Together we made each other's Santa Claus.

This day feels inconsequential without you, maa. No one even wished me last year; in fact, I was all alone at home, crying. I was wondering if Christmas made any sense anymore, as I could feel none at all. The wretchedness of the world was all that I could see as I stared at the ceiling, trying to comprehend if I was even alive. I could feel that I was breathing, but no life lived in me.

People have work, and they get busy, you know. The cracks in walls are often visible, but hearts can be misleading. How do I show them a crack that's deep within, whose surface still appears to be laughing?

I've recently discovered that you must be having the best Christmas ever, with God himself cherishing you. I wish I had made more of those evening teas, more of those cakes and those weird-tasting biscuits. I know you liked them, and cutting the cake made you a baby again.

To my angel mumma, I love you. (Cries in silence.)

11

Dear Death...

I'm crying as my sunshine finds me, making me sober from my last night's hangover. In my time, I gave up my senses.

Oh, I am sorry - I didn't mean to take your mother. But I was too drunk to recognize who I was meant to take. I thought she was the one asking for it, drowning in pain and suffering. Alas, only after it was done, I realise it wasn't her time. I made her feel so helpless. I can only wish to not do it again. I can only wish - because I tell you, the lust for suffering and for being loved in grief, is far greater than your tiny, insignificant feelings and emotions. Cry, my love. Cry.

I'm writing this letter to myself, a record to keep me safe, to remind me to be a little more sober, a little more kind. But every time I think of it, I feel even more cruel. To whom should I be kind? And for whom shall I show respect? To the one who's already dead, to the ones I take with me to life?

I can be colourful, if you see me truly. I come and go as I please, carrying the freedom you crave, unburdened by any responsibilities. I do not care for who's left behind, who asks for me, or who searches me. I come as I please, unannounced, and leave as I wish. Sometimes I spare. And on those occasions, I make better plans. I have a life too, you know.

For a plant to sprout, the seed must break. For you to experience the so-called gift of life, you must die at least once. And oh, I tell you - it's fascinating to kill someone after they've just begun to live. Their joyful, juicy memories make me feel magnificent, just by knowing that I can end it all.

Yet, it is the ones who do not fear me—the ones who dare to look me in the eye—that I like to snatch away the most. The lifeless taste more delicious than living.

Yours truly,

Devoid of Life

P.S., I am still so scared of the girl who was too numb to cry.

12

Swallow.

———♡———

The girl who never cried is sobbing. Her dams have fallen down, and there is flooding. I can't see that. I am a crow, and I can't see tears anymore. I thought I did the right thing—she needed it. She needed to pour out. But every time she sheds, I can feel it.

I never felt this way before. I am a crow; how did I develop compassion? I am black, feathery, dark—something that comes but never truly leaves. But this appears to be foreign habitat, and I want to run away from it.

The eyes are brown, the sea is red. The ruins of my past are ashes everywhere. I have seen people mourn and cry and sob and scream. But I have never seen someone swallow their grief. Please stop doing it, you little girl. Please stop letting it in.

I don't know how deep those ruins go. How will you take them in? You won't just be exhausted—you will be ruined. And I? I have wings. I will fly.

13

I Am Getting My Shit Right.

I am a gentle release, a peaceful breath at the end of a long journey. I am also an intricate chaos - the storm that rips through the world without mercy. I open doors for some with a soft touch, while for others, I slam them shut with the force of inevitability. To some people, I am an angel of mercy. To others, I am the sharp edge of despair.

My eyes tear apart sometimes, watching the pain I bring. But it's my job – to bring that pain because it's the only way to release someone from a deeper suffering. In certain cultures, through sacred traditions, they summon me when the old and frail can no longer bear the weight of living. But when I arrive, they weep, mourn, and grieve the very release they prayed for. Oh, little girl, please cry out. Your tears haunt me – they cut sharper than I ever could. Weep, my girl, for Death itself trembles before the absence of sorrow, where I glimpse the essence of life.

I like to dress up in different forms - an accident on a quiet road, a sudden betrayal of the heart, the slow ebbing of illness. Sometimes, I come soft like a whisper, and sometimes, I strike like lightning. Some slip easy into my arms and some are painfully difficult. The ones that resist, tear themselves apart as I approach - yet eventually, I hold them all the same. I experiment with different guises, sometimes swift, sometimes agonizingly slow. Boredom gnaws at me. Perhaps I should find new disguises, go shopping. A pandemic, maybe? I choose.

You know I can take you to heaven but for your loved ones, it's always hell. Some try to celebrate me, their attempts amusing and strange. But, it's not me who gives them wounds, it's the certainty that they're chasing all the time. I take you away with me for certain, I am the only certainty - oh how hard it is to believe in my permanence! It's not me who hurts them; it's the echoes of living memories. After all, how can death hurt?

It's like lying on the grass, surrendering to the earth, being with yourself and the one who created you. It's the ultimate stillness. It is pure bliss. It is as alive as conception itself.

14

Longing.

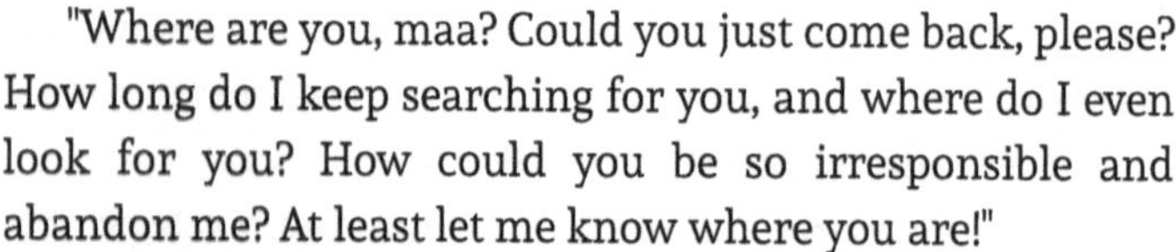

"Where are you, maa? Could you just come back, please? How long do I keep searching for you, and where do I even look for you? How could you be so irresponsible and abandon me? At least let me know where you are!"

I'm right here, see!

"Where?" I growl, "I don't want those clichés of 'living in your heart, close your eyes and feel me.' I want you here, alive!"

Keru, you know that it doesn't work that way. You know it. Don't hurt yourself.

I sob.

"Good night, maa," I whisper, looking at the moon, closing my eyes, hugging her tight.

15

Some Days.

Maybe some days are not about how things are, but how things were.

How I first fell in love with you - the smell of your sweet presence. I guess that was milk. As a baby, I don't remember how you smelled, but as I grew older, I could smell you aging too, Maa. I could trace it in the faint changes of your scent, in the wrinkles that appeared with every secret you kept to protect me. The lashes of life that you endured - they hurt me now, Maa. Some days, things really are about how things were.

Some days, however, are about how things are.

You know, Mumma, sometimes life doesn't feel as miserable as I make it out to be. I feel selfish saying this—how could I ever be happy without you? But the truth is, I do feel content at times. I do look at the mist of pink in the sky, the golden moon, the tender cat, and feel at peace. And in those moments, I can sense your breath, your soul, lingering around me. That alone makes life worth living, some days.

But then, there are days when I loathe the peacefulness of these little things. When the waves of the same ocean, the scent of the same perfume, or the sight of another woman wearing your dress on the street make me want to scream. Cry. Yell—like the way life lashed at you, leaving those freckled wrinkles as a receipt for your love.

Cheers to the joy and misery, the peacefulness and madness that grief offers, maa.

They say souls like us rekindle, but sometimes I wish they never do. I cannot bear the pain of losing you again, nor can I inflict the hurt of those lashes and wrinkles by leaving you in my place. *I hope* we can *die only once.*

16

How Death Was.

Your breaths must have been as clear as this sky, na, Mumma? Visible, penetrating, deep, blue. And your body? Tired, frustrated, angry, and green? How did your lips feel when they tasted death? Slow and steady, or was it too quick, like chilly? Mine feel numb. My fingers know not what they type. The abyss is too hard to describe.

There's fire and a storm. It's rising, and soon it'll blow up like a bomb. The tick-tock is the sound of your death—slow and steady. It arises out of nowhere, comes to my home. How does it know where that is? My body is confused, and my mind runs away. Brain says *error 404*, and the stomach goes to sleep. Eyes wide awake—it's daytime to keep. But how am I supposed to kill this sun that's up here again today? Again and again, this tortures me. Doesn't it know the day is not mine to keep in the darkness that's yours?

Unfair, mistreated, discriminated, glib, empty, fake, insincere, dark, moving—it all feels. When I think of you, Maa—yellow, jolly, vibrant, life is what I see. Balance is so fake, Maa. Life has turned with and without you. How would this river find its way if all they want is bridges around it? They call it protection, but they're putting her in a jail that's not for free.

Shaky, downtrodden, and leafy is how I feel. *Weary* might not be the best word because I breathe. *Dejected* is too simple to see. It's something beyond me—like black after the sun's death, or white in the face of the sun, or violet without the king.

17

Midnight.

Sometimes, it feels like I can't stop breathing, but I would like to. My heart races, pounds, and there's a feeling of something going wrong all the time. It's as if I am losing control over my senses, and my heartbeats. I can't stop thinking and I wake up sweating. It's not anxiety, it's just this immense longing for my soul to be with yours, do you get it?

Sob.

Sob.

Quiet.

Why do you sob?

All these '*what-ifs*' bind me. They make a stickier dough inside me, never leaving without making my hands dirty. It sticks everywhere and makes everything messy. Ew! I want to get this ugly thing out of me, but I fear removing it would mean losing you too. So, I hold on and try to find some comfort in the false hope of your return.

I reach for your arm, but all I feel is my soft penguin's little arm. I could crush it, break it, but I still won't be able to touch yours. I am numb with anger. I can't feel you anymore, I can't hear you. I am afraid that I am forgetting you, Maa. This angers me even more. So, I only keep sobbing. I am scared that one day you will forget me - or have you already?

18
Panic Attack.

I keep staring at the glass ceiling.
It's midnight, and I feel choked.
I try to get up to have some water,
But my body refuses to move an inch.
Suddenly, I gasp for a long breath
And sit straight, trying to breathe again.
It feels like the air has turned to ice,
And I can't find water in this place.
Tears flow down. I feel like I'm going to die.
Suddenly, my hand reaches for the bottle.
Each sip touches every cell of my body,
And I mumble, "Maa!"
I breathe.
I calm down.
This night has passed,
But I wonder—what will I do tomorrow?

19

Blank.

———♡———

Throat quivers,
mouth breathes heavy,
fingers race across the keys,
I see blank.
My head pounds,
my soul aches,
the emptiness inside me waits—
suspended in an abyss of nothingness.
I don't know what could ever be enough.
These noises, these silences,
these places, these pieces of land,
these pebbles, these waters, these spaces—
all grasping at the impossible,
trying to fill just one moment with you.
To be there with you.
To hold you.
To hug you.
To spend just one more second.

20

The Night Never Ends.

The night slips in; my thoughts haunt me. They come, questioning my memories and the waves of quivers that I feel. "Is everything going to be alright?" I ask myself. The silence of the dead creeps in.

The veil isn't as big on the floor as it is on my head. It creeps and crawls all over my ceiling. I fear that a single touch will make the castle of memories I've built fall apart—fragile, even more so than one made of cards. And yet, wave after wave comes in, and this castle remains. I thought memories were fragile, aren't they?

21
Tearing Apart With Memories.

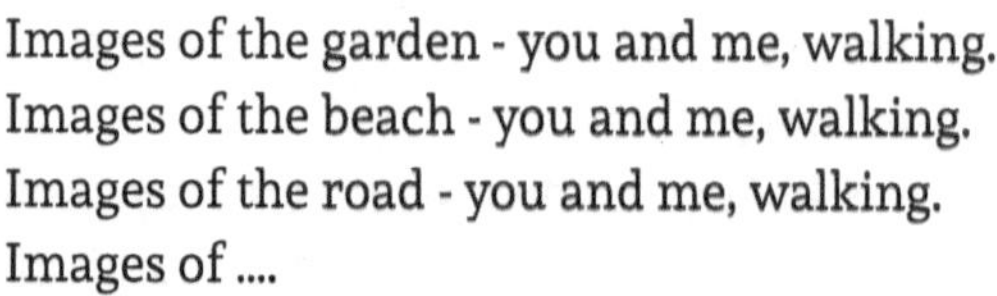

Images of the garden - you and me, walking.
Images of the beach - you and me, walking.
Images of the road - you and me, walking.
Images of ....
Images.

There are times, Maa, when all I can see are the images - the pictures of us being together, holding hands, assuming the world was a good place. But it wasn't the world that was good. It was your hand. It was walking together, in every possible moment, that made love - not God.

I see myself on the swing, my small legs kicking the air, and you behind me, pushing me back and forth. Oh, how lovely it was to be four. But now, two and two make a twenty-two-year-old, yet inside me, there is always a four-year-old.

A four-year-old too hurt and scared to cry. A four-year-old who still can't comprehend what forever means. A four-year-old who still believes that you have become a star - but it is unbearable to see you only at night in the sky, when all she craves is to be with you again, as desperately as God longs to be believed in.

She shouts. She creams. She yells inside. But her eyes show the quiet betrayal of the God the world asked her to obey.

Oh, how could *you really* do this to me?

I don't know what *real* is anymore.

22

How Lonelier Can It Get?

Experiencing loneliness as a daughter grieving her mother isn't just about being in a room with thousands of people and still feeling alone. It's fewer people than that. It's no people at all. No voice to hear, no hands to hold. Even in my own mind, I can't summon a character to bridge the emptiness between the wounds.

Is the wound visible? No.

Is the gap visible? No.

Is the depth of the gap felt, and does it scare the hell out of me? Yes.

I don't even know what this wound is, or how much deeper it'll go. It feels like walking on the moon—vast, silent, barren. There's no one around, just me. In this crater, I am afraid of getting lost. What if I fall, hurt myself, and there's no one to help me up? The last time I fell, you were there to lift me. Who will do that now? I don't have the strength, Maa. Please come home.

I've looked for you on a thousand roads. I'll keep looking for a million miles. I'll keep searching until I take my last breath or until my heart can finally comprehend what has happened. I'll keep looking for you—now and always.

I tell myself this over and over, trying to soften the sting of what they call loneliness. But it's not loneliness. It's the feeling of being a burden to the world, with no one to lean on except the universe itself—because you, Maa, were my living angel.

If not you, then who?

23

Rage.

The mother kicks the ball toward the child. But it isn't just a game—it's as if she's kicking the very spring of life toward her. As I ask myself if I miss those moments, my heart aches to tell you that I don't. It's not the kick I scream for, Maa—it's your feet I want to hold. The ball may come and go, but your love should have been like the sky, ever-present on this earth.

We would have had our stars.

But I didn't always see you as this sky. To the child in me, you were a cold volcano—silent, distant, erupting when I least expected. I remember you as unkind, ruthless, angry. You pushed me. Pulled me. Scared me. You didn't attend to me. You didn't hug me. You didn't kiss me. And that should have made this easier, shouldn't it? It should have been easier to let you go.

Then why does this lingering hope that one day you'll come back and hold me tear apart the stitches I've carefully sewn? Why does this rage sit like a rock in the ocean, heavy with the weight of bearing it all? Why does every breath I take feel like a step further away from you? Why do all colors still blur into shades of grey?

Will this ever be okay, Maa?

24

I Don't Miss You At All.

You're not to be loved, nor to be mourned, nor to be cherished. You're to be held—tight and loose—as you quiver through me. You're to be held as my fingers shake, as this sky cries volumes, as it makes floods in which fishes can't swim, nor can the earth hold. You're meant to be kept, for you were a keeper of me—my entire body, love, and soul.

Your essence runs deep in me, or can I say that I am made out of it? Your blood isn't just red water; it's wine that only nourishes as it grows old. Your grief is like that wine too—only increasing as time goes by, lingering in my life and holding me tight. Some say that I miss you, but boy oh boy, I don't miss you. I long for you, I shatter for you, I ache for you, yearn for you, but no—I don't miss you at all.

Those raindrops feel directionless without you. They are trying to find their ground, but they can't. Gravity doesn't seem to work on this planet without you. It's just like how time doesn't feel like passing, and everything seems like it was just yesterday when you and I called a place home. And now that you are not there, I don't know what home can really be—or is.

25

Trying That Swimsuit and Imagining...

♡

I sat with Death today. Looked her in the eye and asked why. She chuckled—just like my mother would when I'd ask her how she did the things she did.

I am Death. I stared at myself, looked into my own eyes, and sang the song. And there, I found layers in me that surprised me. I appear strong, but in truth, I am a broken mess. Cruel and ruthless at times, comforting and compassionate at others. Isn't that just like you too, Maa?

I saw you try on that swimsuit, layered with blue and your insecurities. I could trace the thoughts racing through your mind—chaotic, like the never-ending rat race of life. I could hear the tear that slipped from your eye and see you hum softly, the breeze of compassion brushing against your face. You kept wondering what I would think, and the silence quivered on your lips.

You bite me every time you see the picture.

26

Maybe Try Giving It To Her.

Many people I take with me have these ideas, desires, and plans they've imagined with their children, husbands, wives, mothers, fathers - God knows who. Why wouldn't you have these plans? But I took them *away*, so what now?

There's a child within you who thinks she can still do things for her mother. Aww, poor you. Maybe you should try doing it for yourself because I provide you with no certainty that the dead hear you, see you, or feel you. No, my child, you don't know what it is after death and you never will. Because once you die, you *die*.

I sound harsh to many people when I ask this, but was she even living before she died? Didn't she die slowly and steadily by her self-made cocoon, somewhere craving for me to come to her - *teasing me* by losing herself? Didn't you see that and mourn? If not, then *why do you mourn now*?

Maybe, you'll run empty if you keep giving to the one who's not there. The hope of having her again will lead you into the abyss of nothingness. Will you ever find her? I won't answer that, because you know the unrelenting truth already. I take away - I don't return. Fear cannot bind me, nor can happiness. I'm faithful to my job after all. But, hey, I do care for the people that I take with me. Unlike you, I free them of the deep pain they carry for years, waiting for me.

Now, with all the guilt in your heart, try giving back to her. I dare you.

27

Trying.

I have been trying to get it right, trying to make it "all right". There doesn't exist a thing called "all right," does there? I long for you and wait for you with every ounce of air that I breathe and every dusty skin cell that I shed. I am trying, Maa, to make myself feel at home, to feel maybe just a little better. But I guess there's no such thing as "a little better" in this period of your absence. Maybe there is nothing that can be made "all right," and that may or may not be "all right".

The picture exists, and only it does. Fragments of memories and pieces of sanity within them appear and haunt me. Turning a year older also means having lived a year closer to your age and a year without you—one more of it, again one at a time. People seem excited about tomorrow, but deep inside, I feel my deadness, as if someone has robbed me of my security and a part of my soul and is not willing to give me an inch of it, even if I tear myself apart to subside in the earth or drown in the depths of an endless, tearless ocean.

I am trying. I will keep trying. One after another, just like how a dead person tries to take her last breath—just like you, I'll keep trying.

28

I Write Sometimes.

All I can see are flashbacks,
Fragments of memory waiting to be a garment.
The closed eyes, the eternal smile,
And the heaviness of yours and mine.
Just yesterday, we were trying to build the castle,
And you snapped out with pipes and pastel.
The white that was meant for the wedding,
Is now a shroud on the winter of you.
Harsh and calm, fierce, and cold,
Storm and sea, nothingness, and wholeness,
Alpha and Omega, dust, and dawn -
All feel the same in your absence.

29

It Wasn't Just Your Birthday.

❦

Sobs.
Sobs.
Holds pen, chuckles - can't write.
Sobs.

30
Back to Basics.

Hm, I can see you cry like the first day.

Oh, wait—you actually didn't do it that day, did you? What were you really thinking? That it's all normal, that everybody loses a parent, so it's okay for you too? Or were you in shock, refusing to believe this was real?

It's not a dream, you idiot. Just wake up and see for real.

You haven't seen your mother for **2 years, 5 months, and 7 days**. Let's make it 8, since it's past **8:47 PM**.

How do you feel?

Oh, cut the crap—hurt, not good, not worth it, undeserving.

Think about it—what did you even do to *deserve* life? Nothing, right? So how can you say you didn't deserve *this*? I know you didn't. But you didn't do anything in the first place. It's simply tragic. Take it.

Stop blaming me for seeing you this way. I was just passing by. I haven't been causing your sleepless nights or your lack of interest in everything. It's my *feathers* you're holding, and that isn't me.

Sure, those feathers hold memories of your mother. The hopes, dreams, and plans you made together. But it's just a wave—you need to crash into it to let it go.

Will you take it?

That wave will drown you. It'll drain you, take away every last drop of blood. It'll hurt like *hell*—it'll feel like the end of the world.

But trust me—you'll be okay. Not in the way you imagine now, but in a new way.

Would you, for once, trust me and take the leap?

Ah.

You're too much of a coward for that, aren't you?

You like these feathers, don't you? The last traces of your blood, your ties, your happiness with her. You're getting *used to* this helplessness, this pity.

Stop screaming at me!

I was just doing my job.

31

Still Waiting For You.

While dusting today, I wondered—does this dust have your particles in it, Maa? Dust is basically skin powder, right? And then, I saw how much had piled up—because we left it there, thinking *you'd do it.*

It punches when my stomach growls, and I don't find you in the kitchen. That's when the painful reminder hits—your absence is real.

Honestly, Maa, sometimes it feels like you're still here. Cooking, cleaning, watching me. Maybe you just stepped out for a bit—to run errands, to get groceries. And then I wake up to that same painful reminder—your absence is real.

I dance to your tunes, but you don't even sing my song. Every time I remember the lyrics perfectly; I think of you—wondering how long it would take for you to remember just one line. I walk into the house and pour two glasses of water, even after two years—one for you, one for me. I cook for four people. I set four plates, four glasses. I talk *about* you, *for* you, *with* you.

Is this all real? Why does the painful reminder of your absence feel so real?

They say they would have died in your place. My brother says it too—wishing he were gone instead, because you didn't deserve it, Maa.

But I would never do that. I could never give you this longing, this pain, this breathlessness, this hopelessness, this grief. I could never be so cruel.

I'm so sorry, Maa. I'd let you go. I'd taken the drift.

After all, the painful reminder of your absence is real.

But sometimes, I wish—more than anything—that it wasn't.

32

Knock.

The morning comes up, and then the moon keeps me company. Thousands of shades change in this sky in a day, but none of them make up to you. How come these million shades are on one end and you on another, maa?

The knife cuts through the chest, piercing everything in between, bleeding out the breath of life. I know that you think this way. Still, I'll knock on your door.

Knock. Knock. Knock.

"I am not playing this joke," you say.

"I am not here to play," I say.

"Go away," you burst out, and I burst in.

I know that I have faded your colours. You sense me walking in.

"Why don't you just leave me alone? Isn't your name in my life enough for you?" you cry.

I don't answer. I just sit with you. You sense this too. Slowly, over layers of anger, we curl up. You scream. I cry.

For once, I beg you to hold me. To let me exist beside you, just for a moment. This job of stripping color away, of swallowing whole the people I love, it guts me too. Please, just look at me once.

Fury fills you. I can see the red beneath the grey.

I know I have been unfair. And we both know it too.

It has been **two years, three months, and 23 days** since I let you see her last. I count them too.

You scream.

Call me what you want—grief, memory, shadow—I only ever wanted to be held too.

33

I Come and Go.

The last time I stepped into your home, you were so desperately lonely. Today, I see you having tea with me. The sky blushes pink, Venus glows orange, and for a moment, it almost feels like old times. You come in with some tea to talk with me.

"Beta, how do I tell you how much I love and miss being with you?"

It tears apart my soul to see you miss me so badly and tell no one because, in the end, you know no one will ever listen to you the way I do. And you won't settle for anything less.

34

Eternal?

Pieces of water fall down. The girl who didn't cry that day now pours out pearls. For once, I see her break in me, and I shatter into pieces. I have successfully done my job of settling grief into this family, but oh, I can't bear to see that girl curl up like me. For once, I find myself being unfair to people. For once, I want someone to mock me as I do. For once, I can feel things.

I am Death, carrying deaths. Since the beginning, I have been doing this. What changed today?

The girl saw me in my helplessness. She pierced me with compassion. She saw the beauty of lying on the solemn grass and ending in the vastness of the sky. For once, I was seen. For once, her mother was seen. Instead of all the made-up stories, she saw a relationship—earnest in all ways.

I found the one thing that cannot die.

35

The Crow Returns.

A mother can never be taken away. She kneads you in her womb and laughs through the billion-bone crack of pain while bringing you into this world. She's the only woman you can never truly be separated from—yet I had the audacity to give her death.

You see, sweetie, it wasn't that I didn't care for her or for you. I cared for us. You were simply getting too comfortable with her, and that was my sign to take her away. How could I let that trust remain between you? How could I not let your heart ache? It needed to—I needed you to live and not die in her life.

I know I must feel cruel to you. Maybe I am. You have seen me laugh while you cried a billion pearls, whispered to me, begged me to undo what I did. I don't feel sorry for you, but I understand your vengeance. I understand your requital. I understand your misery and agony. But you see, it is that blood of yours that keeps you here with me. Those veins are stronger than you'd like to believe.

Your mother is far more alive than dead right now. She isn't with you, but she isn't that far away either.

You just need to learn to fucking communicate.

36

Were You Even Alive Before You Died?

———❤———

Sitting by the desk today, I wondered—would you be happy to see me like this, Maa? Working a job that feels meaningless, just to keep myself afloat. Filling time with music, pretending to reorganize things just to look busy, wasting my skills. And then I remember—you did the same, didn't you?

Every morning, you woke up and did whatever it took to keep us going. To survive. To sustain. And now I wonder—were you even alive before you died?

I see us riding the bike, making up silly songs as we pass Big Bazaar. Singing off-key, ruining the rhythm while you butchered the lyrics. Laughing at ourselves, at life.

Where are those moments, Maa? The ones we chose? For us to cherish each other, to find joy in the ordinary. Driving through the city, giggling, making fun of everything and nothing. I miss just *being*.

Now, there's a clock inside me, ticking 24/7. A to-do list I don't even want to do. A future I bribe myself with, places I don't really want to go. When did this happen, Maa? When?

I'm slowly becoming someone's *maybe*. Someone's *later*. Sometimes, even my own. Is this grief? Or is this just adulthood?

Please, tell me you're coming back. That I can rest my head on your lap and spill the small, stupid, mundane things about my day. Please, Maa. Please.

I can't do this anymore. I just can't.

37

How Come?

———♡———

How come the sun never rose for you again?
How come the moon never smiled at you again?
How come—how come—you never,
never opened your eyes again?
How come the roads never bent for you again?
How come the trees never grew back again?
How come this life is no more again?
Or was it never real to begin with?
How come I never get to see you again?
How come you are eternal, but I remain?
How come our souls shiver together again,
Just to touch—one last time again?
Is it really you, or just my mind again?

38

Stuck.

Roads under construction. Men at work. Traffic at pause. You know what all these mean if you are a veteran of grief. It's always the same, isn't it? You know it is coming, you know when the light goes orange or yellow, you know the triggers, and yet you get stuck. Every time, a new 'stuck', a new traffic, a new work in progress. You know what feeling helpless really is, you know how deeply you long for her.

I know I'd trade everything in a blink of an eye to have her back, but the question really is if she wants to be back or not? This sounds harsh, but to live in that sky, in that infinite of nowhere, I am not sure what my mother would answer. My regret of not saying the last goodbye is the only thing that remains alive in her, in this infinite sense of enormity, this vastness, and this grief.

Those memories are dead in the tunnels of my heart, they wake up sometimes only to let me sleep. They are dead because they keep revolving all around my body, and I know for a fact that they are all alive in each particle that my body holds, breathes, and let's go of. I know for a fact that they sit, they stand, they have fun, and that they evolve into the moments that I cherish and fear for not having just one more. Are we really ever dead?

I have often heard people say to love is to break, but no. To love is to be united in this fog of nothingness, it is to hold tight when the ground beneath you vanishes, when time stretches and collapses all at once, when nothing makes sense but the ache of missing. To love is to exist in that ache, endlessly, helplessly, and still choose to keep loving. It is to be set free.

39

The Motherless Daughter.

—♡—

Engraved upon the thorns, your name lay hidden—
I didn't know it until my head bled.
I didn't know it until my soul shivered,
Screaming from the scars the crown had left.
"Motherless daughter," they call me,
A crown of thorns with a million cuts.
Sharp are the needles of this world—
No one seeks to love, only to bite.
Like a wolf beneath a full moon,
I howl your name each night.
And like moonlight, I wish for you to come,
But these are moonless nights for me—
What will we do now?
Scared, uncertain, I pinch myself.
"Come back to the reality," I say.
But oh, would this body understand—
The bleeding is unseen,
For this crown of thorns is man-made.
Unseen, yet eternal—
Like the motherless daughter who wears it.

40

The Funeral.

I can still see your funeral—how they buried you in the scorching blazes of fire. You were covered in white with rose petals, cotton in your nose. Eyes closed. Wrapped like an offering, a gift for someone so high that we can't touch. At that moment, I felt like I was near the sun, heat blazing up in the cold of monsoon. The day was chilly and grey, as if it was about to rain. The drops that fell were probably a confirmation of losing you forever—for they haven't stopped even today. I guess they never will.

I pick up my phone and call, text, listen to music—do every damn thing to erase the image from my mind. I cursed myself with every blink for even imagining this day, this moment of flashbacks. When I was told that it was real, I felt nothing. Nothing—just like you. Absolutely nothing.

But my body did things. I *vomited*. I *shed* tears and skin. I started staying awake at night. I lost weight. I became lean and weak. I started smelling you. I started losing my sanity. I fumed up, I stayed numb. But God, oh God, I felt nothing. Absolutely nothing—just like you.

Six months later, I felt something while watching a movie. I was only processing the visuals, not knowing what was happening on the screen after that rainy image. It felt like the same day you left. And that something was a tsunami rising from that nothingness. Six months later, I shattered as I said my last million goodbyes to you.

Two years and ten months later, it still feels like losing you was just yesterday. You're still here, aren't you, Crow? Still leaving your feathers behind.

41

No Comfort.

I know that I eat you up—raw and meaty. I know your pain isn't a million miles away but pressed right against you, so close that I can't even cut it. It seeps into every bite of mine, and I am ruthless. I thought I was peaceful, but my feathers are black. They're dark, they're ugly. They only shimmer like a rainbow when you're busy looking around, finding Maa outside you, inside you. But when you search for her in the raw, all you see is this black, mushy tsunami that has lingered ever since the six months passed.

"Why am I like this?" I ask myself at times.

Why am I not peaceful?

Why do I not see the world as you do?

Why is everything blurring and fading?

Why do I keep slipping, one after the other?

Why am I unable to feel?

I wish I weren't a feather. I wish I were comfort—a hug, a pillow soft enough to caress your crown and hold you close. I wish I weren't the thorn but the flower.

Grief is grief. There is no other word for it. And grief is carried over generations. Feathers of grief don't die, for there can be nothing else for grief but grief.

"I know you ache for her. I know she aches for you. There may be no comfort for you—if that ever *comforts* you," Crow stutters.

42

Happy Birthday.

As your existence draws near this planet once more, I feel cold. But not the kind of cold that snow brings—no, the dead cold is different. Snow chills the skin, but death seeps into the bones. It numbs. It overwhelms. It doesn't just linger—it aches.

Nothing will ever be enough. All these achievements, all these feelings, all the daily chores—without you, they feel… meh. My very cells hurt to touch you; they crave your soul. They rise and fall as I breathe, reaching toward the moon. I remember swinging high as a child, trying to touch it. And today, my cells do the same—not for the moon, but for you. You are my moon now.

And just like the moon, you come in phases. Sometimes whole, sometimes scattered. Sometimes luminous, sometimes just a shadow. So are the storms inside my head—some loud, some fleeting. Some crashing, some like deep waters—silent but touching. Your presence wavers between them. Some days, you are a whisper. Other days, a roar. And oh, Maa, I wish I could hold onto the whispers more than the noise. I wish the noise could fill the gaps of whispers that you leave behind.

I fear losing your voice—the way it sounded, the way it smelled, the way it made me feel. I wonder if all the water on this earth could ever quench the thirst you left behind. I still hear the whispers. But will I ever hear you speak again? Or am I left to piece it together on my own, with these storms in my head—storms my soul longs to quiet?

43

Crabs.

We sometimes feel like crabs—out of the ocean, stranded on rocks. As the waves come, we jump in, letting them carry us, hoping to swim through. But what if we are actually fish? How can we survive among these rocks? They hold no love, no kindness, no compassion. They are just what they appear to be—hard, blunt, and black.

Grief is much like a rock soaked in water. It carries bits and pieces of compassion—somewhere more, somewhere less, sometimes stagnant, sometimes flowing. But at the end of the day, it is still a rock—hard, blunt, and black.

They say all colors combine to make white, but in reality, they make black. That is the blackness of this rock. Skinny, uncarved, unclear, yet known. With time, it feels like it has always been there—heavy, stubborn. It tries to hold back the water, but what if it doesn't let it flow at all? It chokes, it wounds, carving out a piece of me one slice at a time.

And then, there's your *love*, Maa—like waves crashing against these stones. Strong, abundant, relentless, but fluid. It never lingers, maybe because I don't know how to hold it within this rock yet. So, when the waves stop crashing, or I find myself dry despite them, I pour out my love through

the eyes that have seen you—both smile and cry.
    Does that suffice? Not really.
    Does that heal? I have no answer to that.
    But I let it come now. These waves feel familiar.

44

Sit.

Maybe on the freezing cold Christmas night, you came to check on me, a furnace to sit by. And I selfishly threw you out, asking you to leave the room as I painted with trembling hands. I was getting it out—the thing built by you. All the *grrrr... aahhh...*

Completing this mess of life, I look at you. Your shadow lingers, your ink seeps through my veins. I dig deeper, but all I unearth is a hollow ache—the kind I have been trying to escape since the last time I saw you.

Finally, I sit with it for a while.

45

Home.

———❧———

Grief is home. A mountain—one not to be climbed, but to be explored. Not a force that isolates, but one that connects. Winding roads with vicious turns, twisting unpredictably, like the way I instinctively reach to catch my falling phone charger—this is home. Not too vast, not too small—just enough to keep me searching.

The lanes dip and rise, leading to a destination called nowhere. A nowhere filled with both belonging and loss. An end, nothing more. Just an end—without you. Hope and joy dance above like the sky, yet I remain trapped under the tree of infinite shadows. It's cold here. The shade protects from the sunlight, but every shadow has its cost.

The roads call to me—they roar, they beckon. And under this sky, my breath steadies in a way it never does beneath that tree, the roots of which run deeper than I can fathom. But I know this sky stretches into infinity. And for now, I will settle for that.

Anger, angst, and scars fade when I see you—vast, towering, endless. Like the leaves, I feel small before you. Not helpless, just small. The mountain is too great, and I grow upon it. I know I may never conquer it. And so, I accept it as my *destiny*.

46
Pieces of Puzzle.

I don't want to go home anymore... because without you, Maa, it isn't home. The thought of it doesn't excite me, doesn't comfort me. Home isn't a place anymore—it's a scattered, fragmented memory, a piece slipping through my fingers like sand. I don't even know where the pieces are, and I'm not sure they'll ever fit together again. Not without you.

To me, home was never just walls and paint. It was where you lived, where you laughed, where you cried, where you danced. It was your presence, Maa—you were home. The sun rises every day, the moon sets every night, but in this world without you, there is no place that I can truly call home.

Now, pieces of you—your memories—flicker around me like frames in an old movie. One moment, I hear your laughter; the next, I feel the warmth of your arms around me. But the moments aren't seamless. They're fragmented, just like life feels now. Like a reel of still images, played fast enough to trick the eye into believing it's real. And my eyes, oh, how they deceive me. They replay those fragments over and over, but none of it fits. It's like watching a life I can no longer reach. And all I can do is let the memories come and go, as tears pour out, as if my heart is shattering with each image.

I'm scared, Maa. Scared that one day, I'll run out of tears. That my grief will flood over, too vast to contain, and I won't know how to hold it back anymore.

I feel like a nomad now, drifting through time and space, never quite settling. I wander through memories, trying to make sense of them, trying to stitch together something that feels whole. But no matter how many times I go back, nothing makes sense. I don't know where I belong anymore. I don't know where to find myself.

Sometimes, I imagine you walking into my room, just like you used to. The afternoon light is soft, the shutters are closed, and you slip in with that familiar grace. You ask me to dance, like we always did, and for a moment, I feel like I'm home again. You take my hand, and together we soar through the sky, weightless. But then I remember—you're not really here. And no matter how much I try, no place will ever feel like home again, because you're not there.

I think a child loses her home the day she watches her mother close her eyes for the last time. I lost mine without even having to watch your eyes close.

I still love to dance with you. I always will.

47

Sunrise and Sunset.

When a baby is born, we celebrate the body—what it can do, the miracles it creates. But when that baby grows up, lives, and eventually dies (I'm not talking about purple babies), we start searching for something bigger, something beyond. We call it a miracle, too, as if we need to believe in them to survive the changes life throws at us.

When you were ripped away from me, Mumma, time stopped making sense. Some days never moved forward, and others stretched so long they felt like lifetimes. Now, the sun doesn't glow the way it used to. Sunsets don't melt into soft orange anymore—they bleed blue, they drown in black. They remind me of all the things I don't want to remember.

People tell me I have my whole life ahead, that I'll find support, that I'll be okay. But weren't you still in the middle of your life, too? How did your night come so fast that the world never even got to see your sunset? Not even me? How am I supposed to believe the sun will rise and set every day when, for me, it's only the moon that keeps me company?

I like how the little stars twinkle in the ocean of the universe. They come, dance tiptoeing, and fade away. They're not afraid of children who look at them and call them their parents, their grandparents, their favourite uncle/aunt, or even friends. They still accompany the child and give them solace. Out of all the haunted-ness of the world, they bring hope—hope to the millions of them, just as they are.

I know that the God who makes the sun rise and set has numbered my hair and your days, both falling at an incredible speed. Maybe if there's anything that travels more quickly than the speed of light, it's grief, your memories, and the hope that one day, in one fine sunset of mine, we'll meet again. Maybe that night, I'll sleep just as I did in your womb—my universe.

48

Sharing.

"Do you ever experience something similar to your mother's love around you?" asked my therapist.

"In bits and pieces," I said. "Once, when my cousin came over about six to eight months after Mumma's death, she wanted to see a photo album from an event that happened when she was probably three or four years old. At that time, we were alone in the room, going through the album. She saw a picture where Mumma was holding her in her lap, and she uttered, 'Mumma.'

I didn't know what to say. I was speechless at that moment. In that split second, I realized how much I had shared my mother with people. My eyes were dry. I looked at her smile—it felt like warm sunshine after days of Kashmiri cold—and said, 'Mumma.'"

Pause.

49

Invisible Wounds.

I can't even cry. Maybe my tears have dried like your body. Maybe they've stopped fighting their way out, like your heart did. Maybe they've given up, like this short span of life that wasn't enough to hold all the love, all the grief, all the missing pieces.

My stomach churns—I feel empty. My hands shake as I type, my brain foggy like a monsoon-drenched mountain. But this monsoon has long since dried, leaving behind the unbearable burn of May. My legs feel numb, like they don't exist at all. I just want to see you one last time. And I'd give up everything for it in less than a blink.

Stop cutting me open with these *invisible* wounds, Maa. How helpless are we—longing for each other, taking the sharp stardust cuts, as countless as the stars themselves?

I feel like I can't breathe. The air is dense, too solid. It's supposed to be light, isn't it? Just like God is supposed to love and protect us. Tell me, Maa—did He make you feel so blunt that you left us without a fight? Or did He love you so much that you chose Him over us? They say love has no boundaries, so I send you hugs and kisses every day. Are you getting them, Maa? Do you feel me the way I once felt you

from inside your womb?
    Do you feel me, Maa?

50

I Wish I Could Say a Yes Again

I wish I could flip the pages and say a yes again.
Empty roads and empty bridges stretch all along.
I want to leave this place, yet I want to stay.
It's you in here, and you out there.
I wish I could go back and say goodbye.
Tears spill with cries and hollow hopes.
Though I know hope is empty,
You're never coming back to this county.
But still, sometimes, I wish things were different.
I wait by the door for you to knock.
But you never come, you never say hi.
All we do is stare by the side and wait.
Wait for broken things to be healed.
Wait for the day when we meet.
Wait for the time we long for.
For once, just once,
I want to eat and sleep in your presence.
I promise—just once.
I know it's foolish to dream the impossible.

And this isn't the motivational kind of impossible.
The world still feels false, like it's playing a trick.
How can you not exist in the world that I'm in?
I love you and hate you at the same time.
I see you as both an angel and a demon.
You come, kiss me, but I still feel empty.
There's a hole within that needs filling.
The hole pains—it's broken.
It's black like never before.
I feel lost and found, anxious and at peace,
All at the same time, in this chaotic piece.

51

It's All Lonely and Dull.

———❤———

I have these questions—*Do I deserve this? Why me?* — and each time, I tear apart a memory made with you.

Not everything *bleeds*, you know, Maa. Some things stay just as they are—stable, unmoving. Like your absence.

I need somebody to hold me, to heal me, Maa. I know that this time, if I fall, it's *the fall*.

Autumn leaves have come, dried, and fallen off. Yet your leaf tries to sprout.

How am I supposed to do this, Maa? What would you do if you were in my place?

Why am I the only one looking for you, Maa?

Are you looking for me too?

Are you coming after me like I do?

Are you trying to reach me in any way?

Are you connecting with me, or is it all just in my head?

Your absence is as white as snow—everywhere in this winter. It's stripping life from the plants, the soil... and me.

How are you so cruel? How can you be?

Your embrace is sweet as honey, your absence sour as lemon.

How could your presence be so soft that my body once danced just thinking about it—yet now, my soul aches at the mere thought?

Are you safe, Maa?

52

Would It Be Enough?

Would these loud noises ever be enough
To fill the silence of my heartache?
Would these lights ever be enough
To brighten the darkness of my soul?
Would these roads ever be enough
To lead me to the place where you are?
Would these clothes ever be enough
To wrap the guilt of not seeing you last?
Would these colors ever be enough
To paint over the black and white within me?
Would these shimmers ever be enough
To hide the melancholy blooming inside?
Would these waters ever be enough
To quench your thirst within me?
Would these longings ever be enough
For one lifetime that trembles inside?
Would all these words ever be enough
To express what I truly feel?
Would these poems ever be enough
To call you back to a place we'd call home?

53

Red.

This red reminds me of the warmth you shared—fleeting yet constant. Like the sun setting in the horizon, yet returning each day. The other side is black, a world of infinite abyss, but your hold is stronger than them all. Even the earth sings your praise. And who am I in this infinite nowhere, spinning on a celestial rock, to refuse the song creation sings of your warmth?

Fading away like the ocean, like my own existence, you move through the room. Not in this moment, but in the vastness of what no longer is. The ache is not just of today but of forever, the stream of you flowing into the generations of my soul.

Are you all those meaningful pinks and greys, Maa? I wonder if the creator who made this beauty, wove you into my mother, only to let you slip away. Is all the red love or anger in the eyes that see? Is grief the only constant my life has to offer? Would there ever be a red that isn't blood?

54

Cold.

The coldness of your feet resembled the coldness of you. We had only just begun to grow warm in this pandemic, and then, once again, you showered your coldness upon me. Attention—a little warmth, a little fuzz—that's all I ever asked for. Was it too much?

I should have seen the crow coming. Didn't I ask you, almost every day— *"Would you ever leave me, Maa?"*

"Where would I go, leaving you?" you'd say.

Well, where are you now?

55

Stitch Between Us.

It's been one hell of a ride, being with you, coming to you. Honey, you push me out a lot, slam the door in my face. But I have a quality all humans envy—persistence. I'll leave my feathers here and there, and they'll remind you of me. They won't let you sleep. You know that too.

Your mother's feet aren't cold. They're cut off. They're dead. Her spring has turned into your autumn. Would you let me in for a while, please? She's not the food; she's the fasting. She's not the spirit, but the alive. She's not the sun and the moon, but you. I come and sit at your inconvenience, but hear me out—I'm yours, and you're mine. No matter if death does us apart. We are not the dumpsters; we are the dumb, trying to stitch words to something as indescribable as the beginning of this earth.

I know her waves crash harder than any rock in the ocean to you. I know the dry reservoirs that have shed enough to never fill themselves again, and yet they pour. I know how my feathers cut through the bare-naked soul of you as you move through this. I know I am fiercer than the winds of the Himalayan treks—for I am, perhaps, an infinite trek myself.

To see you cry, little girl, has broken me too. Aren't we all bound in chains of duty? I wish I could undo my taking. After all, it was your maa I aimed at. Yes, God does make mistakes, and taking her from you was one of them. He is gracious, but his grace has limits too.

56

You Belong With Me.

It's been two years and eight months, and I still ask God for you. I am still overwhelmed knowing that you are with Him and not me. He's probably keeping you safer than I ever could—for He knows all hearts and beats. But does He know how I long for you, Maa?

In this afternoon that searches for itself—just like my spiritual consciousness, lost and seeking—would you be kind enough to grace me? Would you, oh God, accept this written plea to love my mother? How long will You test me and forsake me? How long must I linger in the shadow of a tree whose roots I do not know—how deep, how tangled? How long will I wait for my sun to rise, when every single day, my hope is crushed like a wave reaching the shore, only to break?

You belong with me. You always did. And yet, I still question whether I belong to you. That doubt remains, resting in the abyss of your death—not dark and dull, but cold. Cold enough to kill the heart in me, yet your warmth still lingers, still protects.

I knew you for **20 years, 10 months, and 29 days**—but I do not know how long I will remember you. Maybe I'll die today. Maybe I'll live for a hundred years. But those days, those moments, fill my heart more than the oceans fill the earth, more than the thirst of a crow, more than my own being can contain.

So here I stand before You, Lord, oh God, with a letter in my hands, with an unknown fast of the day, and an unknown desire to see you today. There is so much unknown in me—enough to keep You safe behind walls, enough to shatter me beyond them.

Can I share a little of the known with You today?

How could you sing 'Lag jaa gale' as your last song?

58

Pining for You.

The earth celebrated you on the 13th of January, a Saturday. So will this year. Next Saturday is your birthday, Maa—you would have just turned 51, and I wonder how 51 would have looked on you. Grey hair, runny nose, tons of knee pain? Or the enthusiasm to touch the sky, the hope to travel to Switzerland one day, and feet that comfort like no other? Maybe both would have been you—only if you had lasted long enough for me to see it.

Grieving you also feels like grieving my own self, Maa. This might sound odd to you, but I often wonder what customs and traditions I would have followed, what kind of woman I would have become if you were by my side. Sometimes, things like "just feel her, she's with you" don't really work, Maa—you know it. I do not miss you; I pine for you. I climb mountains and swim oceans looking for you.

Should I celebrate or mourn? Should I sing songs of joy or drown my eyes in grief? 48 wasn't an age to leave, Maa—I was just 20 years old! I am not angry at you, but I am rageful at this universe, at the destiny that decided to bring us closer only to break the gem.

I love you, Maa. And no, I don't miss you. I ache for you.

The crow returns.

59

Howl.

Even in its full greatness, the moon is half tonight. I wonder if you are holding the other half. The northern lights flicker across the sky, shifting like they're waiting for someone, like they're dancing on the fingers of their beloved. I wonder if you are the beloved. Those lights ache inside me, mourn inside me, urging me to remember who I am.

That day, you didn't just die, Maa—I passed away too. There is a *before* you, and there is an *after* you, and nothing in between. I often wonder who I was when you were here and who I have become now that you are not.

The cats grind their teeth while the wolves howl at the moon. I don't know a single moment when my soul hasn't howled for you, anchoring itself to you like its moon. The half that's hidden—*that's* what my body searches for. I wish my eyes could locate it, trace its path, but the constellation of your stars is beyond precious. It's fine, delicate—like the thin line between your spirit and your existence. And I don't know which one to believe yet, Maa. Without you, everything is blurry, like Van Gogh's *Starry Night*—bigger, brighter, more chaotic. And yellow? Yellow is not my color.

Will God ever undo this mistake, Maa?

60

A Bus to Nowhere.

I close these curtains as light floods in. Afternoon, with the sun in glory, cannot reach behind the bark of my tree. The cars rumble over the bridge, and I lie down, waiting to arrive at my destination. Nowhere. No one has heard of it, nor is aware of it, yet I take it for you alone. Will it lead to my wholeness on the way?

I can see the shatters everywhere - those broken quietly like me. They wear helmets. They drive judiciously. They walk nicely. They talk politely. They know they are grieving.

They don't try to be clever - they underplay.

They know what nowhere is and yet don't know how to reach there. They know what wholeness is and are afraid to leave there, coward—just like me.

The Japanese art of mending broken things with gold "kintsugi" makes little sense to me. It's supposed to indicate that scars are beautiful, but no, they are not. They are just what they are—painful and rough, reminders of something once whole. And I know that wholeness doesn't exist without you, so then why do I want to be whole again?

Maybe it's because I've grown up in those buildings full of people with empty families. Maybe I've bred emptiness so much that being full is the only thing I know will keep me safe. Maybe it's because you were my only parent, maa. I'm tired and bored in this only place that I call home.

61

One of His mistakes.

Open fields could not create open people.
God can make mistakes too.
Taking you was one of them.

62

Enough.

A long, long time ago, they said you could never see the sun and the moon together on the same horizon. But I saw them today—the moon, a pale wanderer, circling the giant ball of fire. From dust to root, I've grown in you. Where there was nothing, I found you, and together, we made this dawn come true.

So, living in this world without you feels *out of place*. It's as simple as that. No waves crashing today, no screaming or crying—just silent weeping in the heart. To feel like I don't belong. To feel like I'm a fraud without you. And if someone asks me how I anchor myself, what am I supposed to say? With the living? Or with the dead?

The autumn path holds more weight than the solid spring. If my future is the promise of spring, then I would rather stay in the autumn of my past—where the fallen leaves are no longer scars but memories, broken from the stem of life, resting on the trodden black path ahead. I hope no one ever sweeps them away. They need to stay—to remind this glorious sun and moon that one day, they too will die. Just like you.

Empty places. Children running. Slippers left behind, footsteps fading.

I wonder, Maa, was it painful to nurture me? Did I take too much soil, like this horizon? Or was I cradled in that white wanderer - the moon? Was I like those fleeting free birds, or did I root myself deep like an ancient tree?

Was I ever *enough*?

63

Am I Moving On?

Why does this feel unreal -
To have dopamine shoot in my brain?
Is it okay if I feel a little happy,
In this world without you again?
I'm used to crying silently to sleep
But today, I was not able to weep
My head hit the pillow with a laughter
And I wondered, is this even real?
Does making peace look this way?
Or is my mind playing tricks on me again?
I felt guilty being able to laugh without me -
The me that also left with you.
Is this how life is going to look like?
To laugh and cry more times than I did with you?
I'm not sure I'm ready for it yet
But I guess one day, it'll all fall in place.

64

Why Do I Still Believe?

Would all the snow in the world ever make up for the coldness without you, Maa? These lush green mountains sing songs of praise—how naive they are to adore you without ever knowing you. What difference would it make in this infinity to not have you in my finite-y? I love that cold blood of yours too, for it was cold but still blood. And blood never fades away.

The barren stems of the trees look like they're yearning for your forgiveness. The empty platforms of this train route seem to be waiting for you to fill them. Yearning is not a feeling—it's a calling of the soul, an eternal plea for the impossible. It is the voice of hope wrapped in future falsity, and perhaps these tracks lead to it. Maybe my nowhere is on its way—under the sea, over the sky, somewhere, somehow—because my heart still believes that you exist.

Majestic roars in the distance, empty bridges ahead. Somewhere between these scattered feathers, we are stuck in a life that is neither here nor there. Are we evolving or just bracing against the storm? Is this pain the fire that forges or the heat that burns? I don't know. But I hope, one day, we will find a place we call home. And that day will be the last breath of my eternal hope.

65
Search for Meaning

I'm feeling just as the sky is feeling today—mournful, quiet, wanting to run away. I wonder, where can the sky really run? Into your embrace or into the waters it holds within itself? I can only wonder how things are and how they would have been if you had taken one more auto ride with me in Mumbai, had one more ice cream in the streets of Surat, and shared one last dinner at home. I can only imagine if that one last hug would have made sense to you, somewhere within and around you. Would a hug have saved you from the constant dropping of the ECG meter, Maa?

The sun hangs in the middle of nowhere today, meaningless in its existence among the clouds. I wonder if my grief is the same. I want it to be like these clouds—to have meaning in the end. It's alright if I don't know what that meaning is right now, but I want there to be something. Maybe not all suffering makes sense, but I hope grief is not one of them.

Our vows, like the mist, fade away. We see each other through the fog—so clear, yet so blurred. Your promises have failed, and so have my hopes. Do we make an equal now, Maa? Our actions have buried pain in both of us, yet I stay. Would you please come back one *last* time, Maa?

66

Scattered Roads and Houses.

—♡—

When I was small to grief, it loomed large over me. It sheltered me. It's like freshly grown algae—the more you struggle to move, the more it swallows you in. And you don't know where land is, so you can't even hold on. You just want to get out of it fast.

Death has always been a mystery to us through the ages. We don't know where it leads, and so we want to escape it quickly. But do they—our lost ones—feel like these scattered roads and houses? Here one moment, gone the next. Off the road, lost, untraceable. I don't know. But grief is surely like dried-out grass, fallen and lifeless.

We don't break when we grieve. Living in herds has taught us never to be vulnerable, but oh, how can we belong to a herd when we feel the exact opposite of its intent? How would my body ever feel safe if I carry this around people who don't know it, who don't taste it, who don't see it? Is being invisible really so good?

Harmless are those joys to the infinite, but cruel to this world. "Oh, you're grieving," they say, and then pity. When the universe did not pity, then why do you? None of yours is taken away—it's all mine.

Patient is this vastness, but you will never be. It takes, and it heals. It stands, and it stills. But you would never hold my hand.

Did this surrealness create such a glib?

67
Broken Pieces.

Stones, pebbles, cuts, and bleaches,
Flowing water, war, and wages.
Land, sea, blood, and beaches,
Wood, leaves, fuel, and freezes.
Songs, melody, sound, and noise,
Crow, sunset, dirt, and love.
We, us, you, and I—
Broken pieces of the peaceful move.
Eardrums, silence, flow, and stuck,
Flags, blue, clouds, and sun.
Borders, home, cries, and laughter,
Yet still, broken pieces of the chapter.
Dry, shiver, brown, and dead,
Packed, sealed, thrown, and taken.
Warnings, life, thank you, and sorry—
We won't always be these broken pieces.

68

Grief is a Lonely Place.

Grief is a fucking lonely place to be in. Surrounded by chaos, yet hollow within. People come and go, asking if everything is okay. But how can anything be okay after this? They say they understand, that they know how it feels. But have they really lost someone so close? I've learned that the ones who say nothing, the ones who no longer sob, are the ones who have been to their loneliest place.

Just yesterday, I was lying on my bed, reading a book, thinking. I thought, Mumma will make dinner, and I just have to go and eat it. It's been **two years, two months, and twelve days** since this alternate reality began, yet I still—still stupidly—crave her.

I am done looking for you in the rains and sunsets, in a cup of tea and in songs. I am done talking to your photograph, done convincing myself that the breeze is your hug, that a whisper of wind is your voice. I am done with the make-believe answers in my head, maa. I am done.

I just want you. For real. In blood and flesh.

The sky is deeper than the sea, the ocean vaster than the stars. But my love for you stretches wider than the earth, deeper than the ocean's trench, and higher than infinity itself. And my grief—it is even more magnanimous than that. Because it contains love. Love for you. Love for myself. Love for the past, for the present, for the future, and for all that could have been. Where am I supposed to keep this endless, unbearable ocean of love and grief, maa?

Loneliness is not just an absence—it has depth. Maybe loneliness, like gender, exists on a spectrum. At one end, there are those who are alone and lonely. And at the other end, there is you. You, with all your strength, even with God by your side. But without the one person who, maybe, even loved you more fiercely than God himself. The one who caressed you, cared for you, and stood by you through every storm—without you even calling for her.

Grief is a lonely place. Lonelier than the moon in the night sky, messier than a cyclone's coast. Grief, in its true essence, is discovering an alien connection without tech, without proof, without the alien's awareness of your existence. Grief is like trying to walk on the sun—burning, searing, unbearable.

69

Feathers in Flight

<hr>

You say you cannot heal, yet you hold the threads of your scalp, pulling them down to the fabric of your body. Your ocean hasn't turned to desert yet, but it's on the verge of it. The warmth is drying up as you clutch freckled skin to your bones. There's a cold prickling in the air, as if some witch is handing it out for free. Did she steal your warmth, hoarding it in her bag? Did the coldness of your death not warm the world around it, that it still aches even today?

Maa, oh Maa, how long is this wait going to be? Those photographs sit silent and dead, yet they scream of warmth, of light, of the golden strands in my hair. Am I never to feel that again? Would you really rob me of these memories, these scars, and take them away just like death took you? I still can't believe what has happened. Won't you make it easier with a hug, a kiss? Isn't that enough to mend a miss?

And you—your feathers are a mess around me, you crow! They are not black, not dark, but grey like my old Nani's hair. They've taken flight over and over again, yet they are fresh in their experience. They know what they do. They love to wrench my heart, to drain me. I wonder if they're vampires who thirst for my blood and flesh, or if it's just your claw, pricking at my longing.

70
Between Silences and Storms.

Are you in these flowing waters,
Or hidden in the majesty of the mountains?
Are you in the endless chatter around me,
Or in the sound of that silent, still water?
Are you in the magnificent trees,
Or tangled in the thorns of that lonely shrub?
Are you in the untouched white snow?
Or in the darkness of my long, black nights?
Are you in these sharp, biting pebbles beneath my feet,
Or buried in the sand that cradles forgotten weapons?
Are you in the life that breathes within the water,
Or in the stillness of the dead, within this endless noise?
Are you in those fleeting moments of laughter and tears,
Or in the fragile bridges swaying on the edge of the mountain?
Are you in the boundless universe above,
Or lost in the depths of these words that fail to capture meaning?
Tell me,

Are you even alive?

71

There is something about you that my restless heart is beating for today. Something in that crescent shape of yours, surrounded by just one single, naked star. Is that how lonely this grief is supposed to feel? Is that why, when a star comes near me, I hold it so tight that it chokes to death in my grasp?

72

For an Infinite Number of Times, YES.

I kept staring at you—at those round cheeks and innocent eyes. But they weren't quite innocent; they carried the burden of age and the child within you. The child that wanted to be free. You spoke of Switzerland, and your eyes shimmered, as if some peaceful wand there could magically make you happy.

"Are you happy, Maa?" I asked.

"If you are happy, then I am happy," you always said.

Sitting here now, with the same eyes of a child and the burden of an adult, I ask myself if I am happy. But little do we know—answers like these do not exist. Maybe now I understand what feeling lost truly is. Maybe Switzerland was that one place that gave you peace, a place you believed in, a place that held your hope for me to find you again. But would I really find you in the Swiss mountains, Maa? Would I ever be able to see what you saw? Round cheeks and innocent eyes—did they ever lie? Earth isn't the best place to live... so is heaven where you go?

You looked back and said, "Stop looking at me like that! What's there?"

I kept staring and smiling. I fancied you.

Now, my soul understands why I kept looking at you like that. I was clicking photographs of you in my mind, immersing myself in the nectar of your soul, knowing that one day, I'd have to synthesize my own honey. Did it have to be this soon, though? Couldn't you have let my wings mature a little longer?

It's not the big things that I look for you in. It's that stare, that round cheek, and those innocent, burdened eyes that cut me a thousand times every time I think of you. And I wonder—will there ever be a moment when I don't think of you?

Will I keep staring at you still? Yes. For an infinite number of times, *yes*.

73

Itch.

It's been ages since I last saw you. Faded memories, tinted glasses remain. Like the wings of a butterfly—intrinsically delicate—so are my neurons when it comes to you. Am I forgetting how you sounded, how you looked, how you smelled, how you tasted?

We did not share the best relationship, Maa. Our own itches fought against us. They echoed within us as we sat in silence—just like this lingering hope of seeing you one last time. Memories fade, leaves fall, people grow old, but your cruelty remains. No towel can dry it from the wings of my heart, and no warmth other than yours can mend it.

We had only just begun to make each other feel loved. I wonder if I was ever the kind of child you'd look back at and claim as yours. Lights flicker like moments today, and I try to hallucinate you—for that is the last trace of a mother I may have. Can we really take it any further now?

I'm holding on, but I don't know for how long, Maa. Maybe a lifetime. Or maybe until the crescent moon in the sky, waiting to be full—cut and broken in its vastness. I don't know what sounds less like you anymore—my screams or my laughter, my tears or my silence. This body feels like a traitor. I'm not sure how long I can hold it.

74

In the Beginning.

Beginnings are always chaotic—filled with a whirlwind of ideas colliding with a void of nothingness, feelings crashing together like a storm. My beginning is no different. This chaos feels universal. I stand here, paralyzed, unsure of where to start, grappling with a tangle of plans that seem hollow. The first draft of my grief feels lifeless. Contrary to that, the first grief is rarely dead, it is raw and pulsating especially when it is for a parent.

People say the death of one's own children is the ultimate grief, but I believe that all griefs are ultimate; they test more than a person, they test the essence of the soul. And oh, how fragile is this soul!

Running away, fading into oblivion, facing it head-on, running towards the storm, walking through it, or just freezing still. I don't know how it goes. It's different for everyone but I guess not so different after all. No one understands it.

The images haunt me. They creep into my thoughts, twisting my reality, shaking me to my core. Above all, your existence terrifies me. I don't know what to believe anymore, the moments I spent with you or the imagined fantasies and agonizing 'what-ifs' that torment me. Were you really living when you were alive or were you dead long ago, maa?

Loving you wasn't so hard, it still isn't. But believing in your existence feels like the ultimate struggle – a fight for life itself.

75
Finale of Reality.

I don't think I'll ever be able to finish this, Maa. No number of words could ever do justice to the grief I carry every day. I don't think there will ever be a day when I won't say your name, when I won't talk about you. I don't think this grief will ever end.

I'm stuck. Stuck on the day of your death. Stuck on the last time I saw you alive in that hospital bed, dropping you off for treatment. Stuck on the moment I heard the finality of your death. Stuck between these shades of sky, searching for you. I think I'll always remain stuck—just as water will always keep flowing in the river, no matter how much of it. I think I'll always remain stuck, like salt in the ocean, until I become one with this stuck-ness one day.

The autumn leaves will fall, making way for spring to bloom, but I will always be in winter. It will always snow and blow cold, like your feet in that hospital bed. There will always be a part of me that is dead with you. There will always be a long list of possibilities that died with you. I'm not sure what I miss more—you, or the moments we could have made.

I wish I could gather these feathers of Death and keep them hanging with me forever. I wish nothing would ever make sense, that I would always remain stuck on that day. There is an unknown comfort in the dark and cold, and I guess I am more familiar with it than a spring without you. I don't know if any of this makes sense, but I sincerely hope the crow never knocks on your door.

www.ingramcontent.com/pod-product-compliance
Lightning Source LLC
Chambersburg PA
CBHW031735150726
47989CB00006B/2475